Do-it-yourself
Face Painting Book

by
Michel Malherbe

What you'll need:

* You'll be able to find most things mentioned in this book in a toy shop.
* Make-up sticks or special water colours. Don't use ordinary water colours because they can cause skin allergies.
* A black pencil with a soft lead will help you draw in the basic lines on the face.
* Adhesive stars and glitter.
* A fine and a broad brush if you're using water colours.
* About four sponges, cotton buds, gauze bandage and tissues. Foundation. (Ask your mother if you can borrow some of hers.)
* A comb, a brush, hair grips, hair gel, soap and a towel. For general instructions: see the last page.
*

BALLOON BOOKS

A Rabbit

Tame rabbits have soft fur and are affectionate pets.

Here's what you need to look like a rabbit:

- pink foundation
- white, black and pink make-up

- rabbit's ears
- white T-shirt and tights
- a yellow pompon for the rabbit's tail

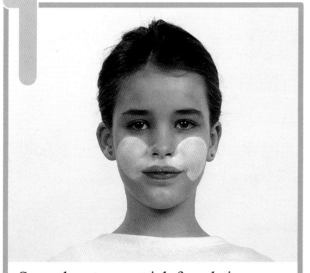

Smooth out some pink foundation over your face. Colour your cheeks and top lip white. The white cheeks should come a little below the corners of your mouth.

Draw in black semi-circles from your eyes to above your eyebrows. Draw a fine black line under your eyelids.

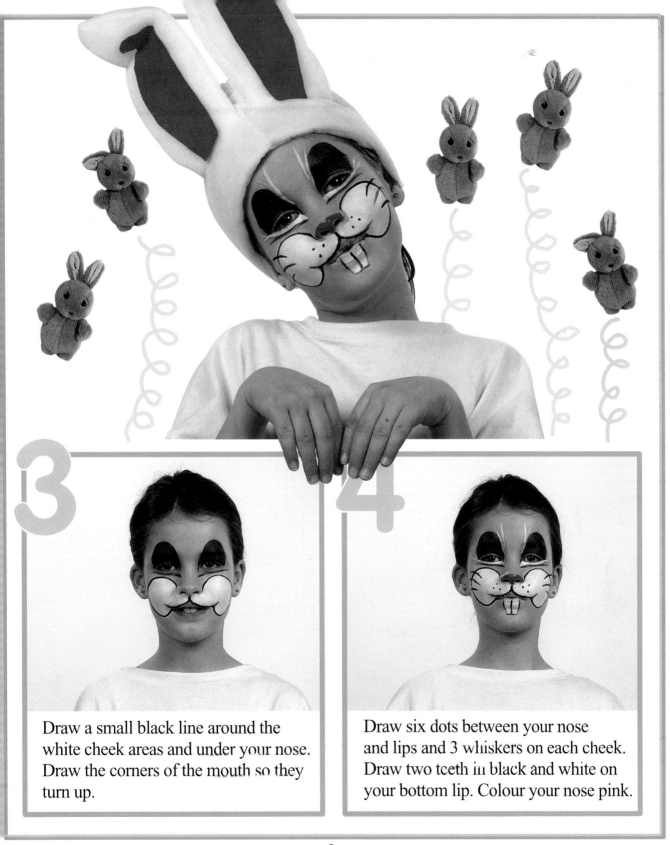

3 Draw a small black line around the white cheek areas and under your nose. Draw the corners of the mouth so they turn up.

4 Draw six dots between your nose and lips and 3 whiskers on each cheek. Draw two teeth in black and white on your bottom lip. Colour your nose pink.

A Brown Bear

Teddy bears can be adorable cuddly toys, but real bears can be extremely dangerous.

Here's what you need to make yourself look like a bear:

- brown foundation
- white, black and red make-up
- bear hat with ears
- something you can put on in bearskin

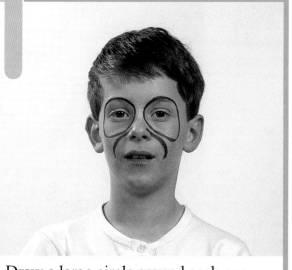

1 Draw a large circle around each eye, from just above your eyebrows to your cheeks. Draw a line from your nostrils to the corners of your mouth.

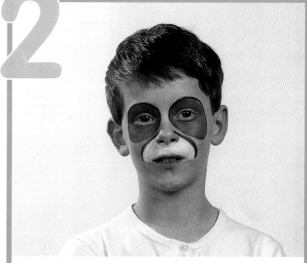

2 Colour the circles around your eyes red. Make the area between your nose, mouth and black lines white.

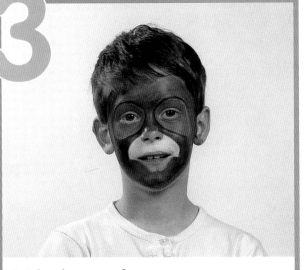

3

Make the rest of your face dark brown, except for the tip of your nose and lower lip.

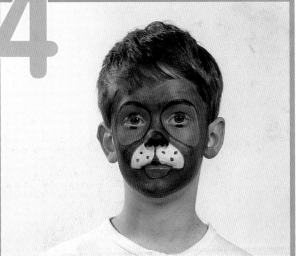

4

Colour the tip of your nose black. Draw six spots on the snout you have drawn and colour the lower lip red. Draw a fine black line above and below your eyes.

A Wicked Witch

*Everyone knows that witches are wicked and ugly.
Wouldn't it be fun to be
a horrible witch at a party?*

Here's the things you need to make yourself look like a witch:

- green foundation
- black, green, pink and brown make-up
- sponge
- a witch's hat
- a large dark shawl
- a broomstick
- soap

Using a sponge, spread a little green make-up as a foundation over your whole face. Put some soap mixed with a little water on your eyebrows.

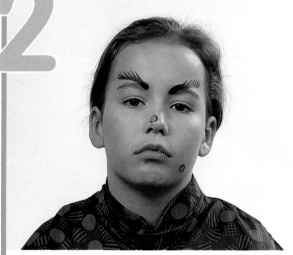

Using a black make-up stick, draw in some high, thick eyebrows. Warts are growing on the nose and on the jaw. Colour the inside of the warts darker.

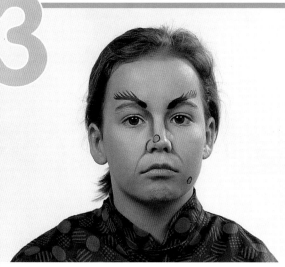

3

Using a brown make-up stick, colour the sides of the nose dark. Draw wrinkles from the nostrils to the corners of your mouth.

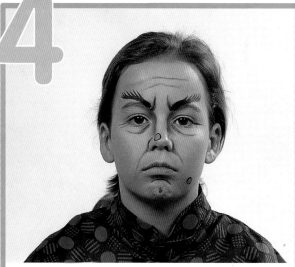

4

Draw lines on your forehead, above your nose, under your eyes and above your chin. Draw a mole on your chin.

Pierrot, the White Clown

Pierrot is a sad clown, but he always manages to look very clean and tidy.

Here's what you need to look like Pierrot:
- white foundation
- black, blue and pink make-up
- small silver star
- a white ruff
- a white T-shirt
- a black hat
- soap

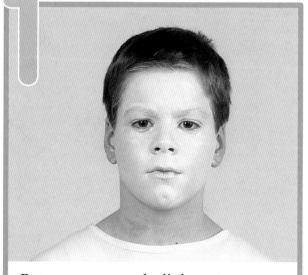

Put some soap and a little water on your eyebrows. When the soap is dry, make your whole face white, including the eyebrows.

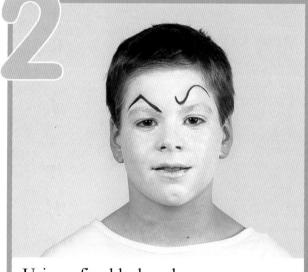

Using a fine black make-up stick, draw a "roof" above one eye and a "horizontal S" above the other.

Paint small but thick lips with a pink make-up stick and draw a fine, black line along the edge of your lips.

Close your eyes one at a time and paint a black circle on each eyelid. Draw a tear on your right cheek. Stick a small star on your left cheek.

Joey, the Merry Clown

Joey is the best known of all the clowns.
You often see him in the circus. He's a bit clumsy
and stupid but always making people laugh.

Here's what you need to look like Joey:
- white, black and
  red make-up
- soap

- a wig
- a big bow
- a small funny hat

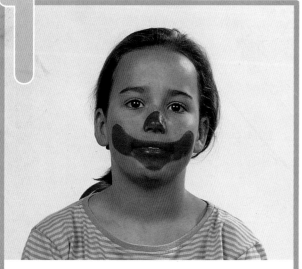

Draw a big red mouth, stretching almost from ear to ear. Also colour your lips and the lower half of your nose red.

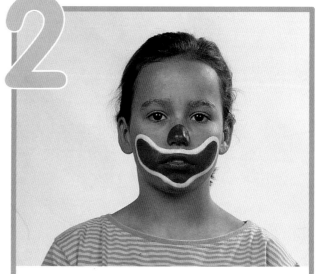

Using a white make-up stick draw a thick line around your mouth. Make sure that the corners of the mouth you draw are curving upwards.

Rub soap and a little water into your eyebrows and wait until the soap is dry. Using a white make-up stick fill in large, half-oval areas around your eyes.

Draw a thick black line above each eye. Draw eyebrows along the upper edge of the white areas. Draw a black dot on each cheek.

A Dangerous Pirate

A pirate's face is really great for a carnival celebration. You'll be a super hit if you can put on a really 'cool' look as you glance at everyone.

Here's what you need and the accessories to look for:

- sponge
- black and red make-up

- a striped T-shirt
- a spotted scarf

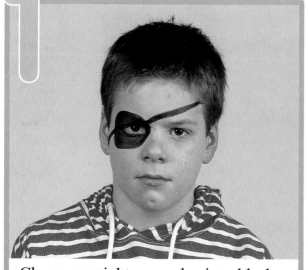

Close your right eye and paint a black patch. Draw a black line from your right ear diagonally across your black patch up to your hairline.

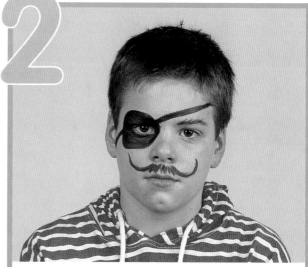

As finely as possible, draw a short-haired moustache. Draw the points of the moustache in an exaggerated curve upwards.

3 Using the black make-up stick, rub it carefully over a hard sponge and press the sponge against your chin and jaw until you have a stubbly beard.

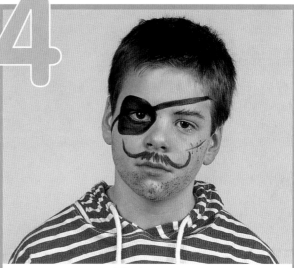

4 Draw a scar with the pink make-up stick on your left cheek. In the middle the scar should be thicker and darker. Draw 3 lines across it for the stitches.

A Friendly Cat

A cat is the most popular pet.
It is very affectionate but likes
its independence.

Here's what you need and the accessories to look for:

- black, pale blue,
  pale green and red
  make-up

- cat's ears
- black sweater and tights
- a long tail

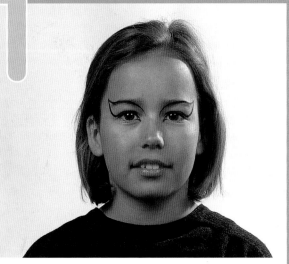

Using a black make-up stick draw attractively curving eyebrows and connect the outside corners to the corners of your eyes.

Colour the lower half of your nose and a small area down to your upper lip red. Also colour the middle of your lower lip red.

3

Draw a black line above the red nose, then 3 straight lines for whiskers. Colour the upper lip black with 2 lines extending upwards to your nose.

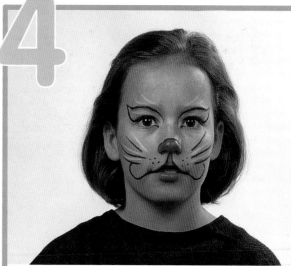

4

Draw pale blue lines between the whiskers. Above and below your eyebrows colour in some pale green shadow lines.

A Princess

Many girls dream of going to a party dressed as a beautiful princess. If you follow the steps below, you can make your dream come true.

Here's what you need and the accessories to look for:
- pink foundation
- white, black, red, pale mauve or silver make-up

- small stars and glitter
- a splendid crown
- some white voile

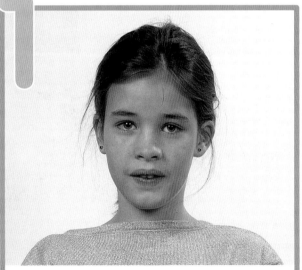

Using a make-up stick and a sponge smooth pale pink foundation over your face. The edges of your face should be darker than the rest.

Colour your eyelids white and draw black eyebrows curving upwards. The outside edges should end in a point.

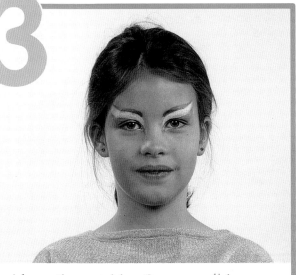

3 Along the outside of your eyelids, alongside the white, colour a shadow, using the silver or pale mauve make-up stick.

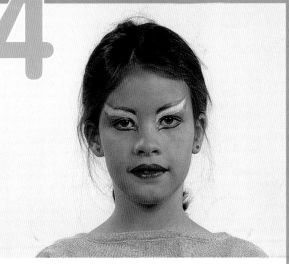

4 Using the red make-up stick, colour your lips. Stick 2 stars on to each cheek and add some glitter above your eyebrows using a sponge.

A Magician

*Everyone would like to be able to do conjuring
tricks, so we're a bit jealous of the magician.
That's why we enjoy being a magician at parties.*

Here's what you need to look like a magician:

- light brown foundation
- black, brown and
  white make-up
- double-sided sticky tape

- a black beard, moustache
- a magician's hat
- a magic wand
- coloured circles

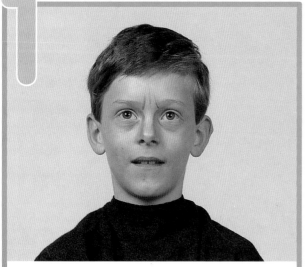

Make your nose look narrower by
colouring light brown shadows along
each side and draw in wrinkles between
your eyes.

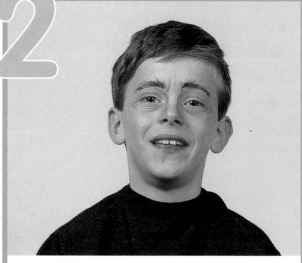

Colour black, bushy eyebrows
and draw brown wrinkles in
the corners of your eyes and
under your eyes.

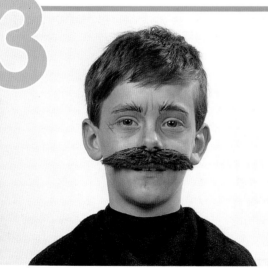

3 You can usually find black moustaches and beards in a toy shop. Using a white make-up stick, make careful marks on the hairs until they look grey.

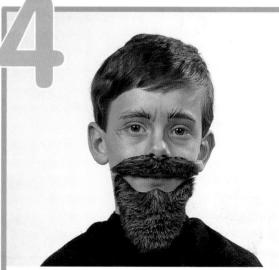

4 Attach strong double-sided tape to the back of the beard and moustache. Fix them in position on your face.

A Japanese Geisha

Geishas are specially trained so that they are always friendly and patient. They also wear make-up to make them look as beautiful as possible.

Here's what you need to look like a geisha:

- white foundation
- dark red, black
  and red make-up

- a kimono / dressing-gown
- white scarf
- a pair of knitting needles

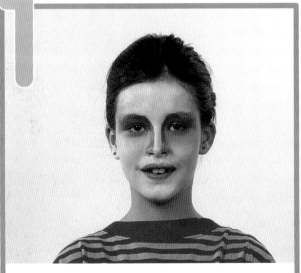

Smooth a foundation layer over your face with a white make-up stick. Colour shadows above the eyes and along the sides of your nose with the red stick.

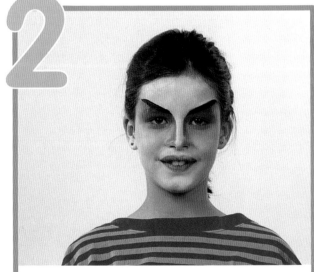

Draw thick black eyebrows running diagonally upwards, ending in a fine point.

3 Draw a black triangle from the outside corner of your eyes towards the temples. The line should end in a point. Under the eyes draw a line to reach your nose.

4 Colour your lips dark red. Make sure that the lips and corners of your mouth end in a fine point.

21

A Colourful Jester

The jesters were the predecessors of the clowns and jugglers. In the Middle Ages they performed in fortresses and castles.

Here's what you need to look like a jester:

- white, black, blue, red, yellow and green make-up
- jester's hat
- bells
- jolly clothing

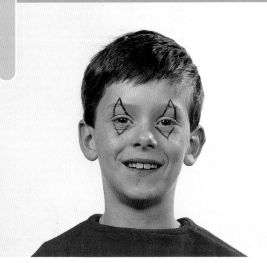

Using the black make-up stick, draw triangles above and below your eyes, from one corner to the other, forming a diamond around each eye.

Draw large circles around your eyes and colour the area between the circle and the diamond completely black. The circles overlap above your nose.

Close your eyes and colour the diamonds white. Draw three more diamonds on each cheek and paint them different colours, blue, green and red, for instance.

Colour the triangle between the sides of your nose and the diamonds yellow. Colour your lips red and draw a black line along the edges of your lips.

General instructions

1. Before you apply the make-up, it's better if you first put a layer of not-too-thick foundation over your face. Spread it smoothly over your face using a sponge.

2. Look carefully at the example in the book for every line and every area.

3. If you want to hide your eyebrows you'll need to apply some soap and a little water first to provide a greasy surface. Leave it to dry before putting on the foundation.

4. Make sure you're sitting in front of a large mirror. It's important there's plenty of light too so that you can see what you're doing.

5. Use hair grips or hair gel to prevent your hair from falling on your face.

6. Once your make-up is finished you'll also need to wear clothes to complete your transformation. You're sure to find things you can use in your wardrobe. A pirate would look good wearing a black or white T-shirt or a red-and-white striped one. Sometimes you'll need to make something yourself from old fabrics or packaging material. Look carefully at the photographs in this book and then think up some ideas of your own.

7. The make-up can be removed quite simply, using just tissues. Water colours can be washed off using soap and water.

With thanks to Silke Helsen, Wouter Koops, Maria Cristina Alegria and Jeroen Reymer for their patient posing for many long hours.
Photographs: Diapress